LOOK

I'm a Cook

For the grown-ups

This book is full of hands-on play activities and recipes that will tap straight into your child's natural curiosity. Each activity is designed to let your child play and learn with all their senses. Together, you can grow their love of food, cooking, and science, as well as their understanding of the world.

Here are a few tips to help you along the way:

Your child should be supervised at all times when cooking and experimenting, but try to give them time and space to lead the direction of play. The questions in this book are suggestions. Let your child ask, and answer, their own questions.

•

Involve your child in each step of the recipes. Let them measure, mix, and follow the instructions. Encourage your child to taste as they cook, and allow them to modify the recipe if they would like to.

•

Adult Alert stars show where your child will need extra grown-up help. Before you start cooking, consider any kitchen hazards together and ways to avoid them. If your child has long hair, make sure it is tied back and out of the way.

•

Protect the area where your child will be playing, and encourage them to wear old clothes or an apron. Being prepared lets your child enjoy themselves to their fullest. Making a mess is part of fun and learning!

Adult ALERT!

DK | Penguin Random House

Editor Hélène Hilton
Design and Illustration Rachael Parfitt Hunt
US Senior Editor Shannon Beatty
Additional Design and Illustration Charlotte Milner
Educational Consultant Penny Coltman
Photographer Dave King
Food Stylist Denise Smart
Jacket Designer Charlotte Milner
Jacket Co-ordinator Francesca Young
Editorial Assistance James Mitchem, Marta Rybarczyk
Design Assistance Eleanor Bates, Charlotte Bull, Rachael Hare, Pauline Korp
Pre-production Dragana Puvacic
Production Amy Knight
Managing Editor Penny Smith
Managing Art Editors Mabel Chan, Gemma Glover
Publisher Mary Ling
Creative Director Jane Bull

First American Edition, 2017
Published in the United States by DK Publishing
345 Hudson Street, New York, New York 10014

Copyright © 2017 Dorling Kindersley Limited
DK, a Division of Penguin Random House LLC
17 18 19 20 21 10 9 8 7 6 5 4 3 2
003–299879–June/2017

Published in Great Britain by Dorling Kindersley Limited.
A catalog record for this book is available from the Library of Congress.
ISBN: 978-1-4654-5964-0
Printed and bound in China

The publisher would like to thank the following for their kind permission to reproduce their photographs:
(Key: a-above; b-below/bottom; c-center; f-far; l-left; r-right; t-top)

21 Getty: Photographer's Choice RF/Jon Boyes (cr). **25 Fotolia:** Eric Isselee (cr).
All other images © Dorling Kindersley

For further information see: www.dkimages.com

And a big thank you to all the little chefs who acted as models: Clara Fox, Thomas Hellyar, Eddie Hunt, Elijah Knight, and Liyah Ventour-Russel.

A WORLD OF IDEAS:
SEE ALL THERE IS TO KNOW

www.dk.com

Contents

Little minds have big ideas!

You don't need a **tall white hat** or a **fancy restaurant** to be a great cook. You already have everything you need: **your brain** and **your amazing senses**!

Curious questions

Cooking is so much more fun when you experiment. Here are some questions to ask yourself as you cook.

- How does my food look, feel, smell, sound, and taste?

- What changes do you notice in the food when you follow the recipes?

- Why do you think the ingredients change as you cook?

- How can I make food taste better?

Your cooking senses

Brain
Your brain is not one of your senses, but it gathers information from them all and tries to understand it.

Hearing
Cooking causes lots of interesting sounds. What can you hear?

Sight
Food should look yummy as well as taste good!

Smell
Lots of the flavor of food comes from its smell. What clues can your nose give you?

Taste
Your tongue is your best chef's tool! Try your food as you cook it. Does it taste as good as it looks?

Touch
Your skin tells you how things feel. Be careful with objects that might be hot, cold, sharp, or that might hurt.

Let's see what we can do!

Play with your senses

When you eat, **all your senses** work as a **team** to tell your **brain** about what you're eating. Try these **kitchen experiments** to find out how **important** each of your senses really is.

Taste

Your **tongue** is covered in little bumps called "**papillae.**" Inside the papillae are lots of **taste buds**. Your taste buds let you taste **different flavors.** Can you see your **papillae** in a **mirror**?

Children have more working taste buds than adults.

Look at your tongue in a mirror.

Sight

Your **eyes** give you clues about food before you eat it. Wear a **blindfold** and **try** different foods. Can you **guess** what you're eating **without seeing it**?

Smell

Your sense of **smell** is even more sensitive than your sense of taste. Try **smelling** an **onion** before taking a bite from an **apple**. Does it change the **taste**?

Touch

The inside of your mouth can **feel** the different **textures** of food. Eat a **soft** slice of bread and a slice of **crunchy** toast. Which do you like **better**?

Hearing

Lots of food makes **sounds** as you **chew** it. Try eating **crunchy** food with your **hands over your ears**. Does this make a difference to the way the food **tastes**?

7

Strawberries grow big and red in the sun.

Sunshine strawberries

Lots of our **food**, such as **fruit** and **vegetables**, comes from **plants**. Can you guess where these **ingredients** have come from?

Makes 4 bowls

You will need:

10oz (300g) strawberries

4 tablespoons honey

Honey is made by bees. Bees work very hard to make honey from flower nectar.

You can grow strawberries in your garden or in a flower pot.

2½ cups yogurt

a few mint leaves

8

1

Wash the **mint** and **strawberries** with cold water.

Oops! I've lost my hat.

Adult ALERT!

2

Remove the **stalks** and cut the **strawberries** in **half**.

Strawberries are full of vitamin C, which helps your body fight germs.

9

3

Can you smell the mint?

mint

Tear the **mint** leaves into teeny tiny pieces (as small as you can make them).

> Yogurt is a good source of calcium, which helps your body build strong bones and teeth.

4

Spoon the **yogurt** into 4 bowls.

smooth

and silky

> Strawberries and mint are plants, but most yogurt is made from cows' milk.

drizzle

Yay! I made it!

Rabbits like mint as a treat!

5

Divide the **strawberries** and **mint** between the bowls and top with **honey**.

11

Greenest guacamole

Guacamole is made from **mashed-up avocados**!
It's a fresh, creamy, and **very tasty** recipe.

You will need:

2 medium tomatoes

handful of cilantro (if you like it)

half an onion

3 ripe avocados

half a lime

salt and pepper to season

Wash the tomatoes and cilantro before using them.

1

Chop the **tomatoes** and **cilantro** (if using) as small as you can. Carefully grate the **onion** with a cheese grater.

When you grate or cut onions, they release a gas that makes your eyes water.

Adult ALERT!

chop chop

scoop

2

Cut the **avocados** in half around the pit. Remove the pit and **scoop** the soft insides into a bowl.

Avocados are great for keeping your heart and brain healthy.

13

mash

Mashing the avocado gives it a slightly chunky texture.

3

Mash the **avocados** using a potato masher.

4

Add the chopped **ingredients** into the bowl and mix everything together.

Mix it all up!

5

Finish your guacamole by squeezing **lime juice** into it. **Season** with salt and pepper, then mix and serve.

SENSE-ible cooking

- How does it feel to mash the avocado?
- Does the avocado change color?
- Does the lime juice taste sour and acidic?

Sour science

Lime juice helps your guacamole stay **bright green**. Without lime juice, avocado turns **brown** when it touches the **air**. That's because the avocado **reacts** with a gas in the air called **oxygen**. Lime juice is full of **citric acid**, which **slows down** this reaction.

Citrus fruits all have citric acid in them. You can taste it—it's sour and might make you scrunch up your face! Which one of these citrus fruits tastes like it has the most citric acid?

orange

grapefruit

lemon

lime

blood orange

Salad train

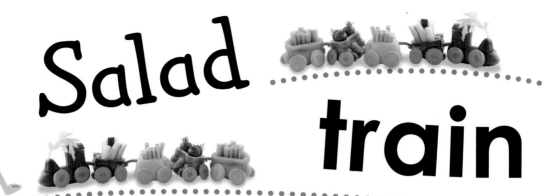

Vegetables come in all **shapes**, **sizes**, **colors**, **textures**, and **tastes.** Make them even more **exciting** with this recipe. All aboooard! **Choo! Choo!**

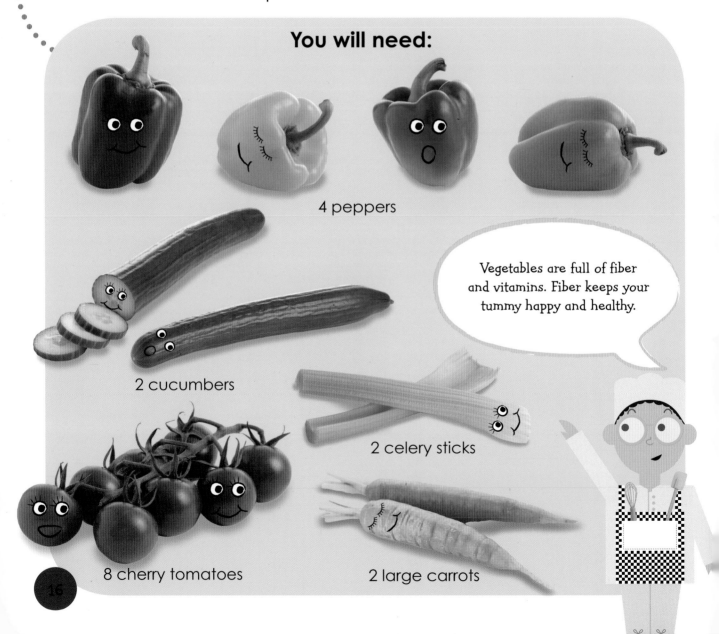

You will need:

4 peppers

2 cucumbers

Vegetables are full of fiber and vitamins. Fiber keeps your tummy happy and healthy.

2 celery sticks

8 cherry tomatoes

2 large carrots

16

1

Wash the vegetables with cold water.

splash

2

Carefully **peel** the carrots. Then cut the celery, 1 cucumber, and 1 carrot into chunky sticks.

Be careful!

Adult ALERT!

Serve with your guacamole dip.

Time to make your **train**

guacamole

3

To make the **train cars**, slice a side off the peppers and **scoop** out the seeds with a spoon.

Yay!

Fruit and vegetables both come from plants.

4

Fill the pepper train cars with the vegetable sticks and cherry tomatoes.

SENSE-ible cooking

Which vegetables have bumpy skin and which ones feel smooth?

Can you hear the vegetables crunch as you bite them?

Do all the vegetables taste the same? Which is your favorite?

Use carrot slices for wheels.

Make the front from cucumber and add celery leaves to look like steam.

All aboard!

Can you remember the names of all your ingredients?

Buggy feast

Some **plants** hide their **seeds** inside **colorful fruit**. Fruit tastes **yummy** so animals eat it and **spread** the seeds. Fruit is also great for making amazing **little creatures!**

You will need:

Try using herbs, icing, and chocolate chips to add faces and details to your creatures.

1 apple

1 apricot

a handful of grapes

1 tangerine or orange

1 kiwi

half a banana

Remember to wash your fruit.

Red ladybug

To make the body, cut a **red apple** in half and remove the core. Add a **grape** for the head and use **icing** to stick on **chocolate chips** for spots.

Summer sun

Peel a **tangerine** and arrange the segments around half an **apricot** to make a sun.

Busy butterfly

Peel and slice a **kiwi** for wings. Use an **orange** or large **tangerine** segment for the body, and use **mint** for antennae.

Snazzy snail

Draw an icing swirl on an apple slice to make a snail shell. Use half a **banana** to make the body and add **mint** antennae.

Cute caterpillar

Carefully push **grapes** onto a wooden skewer to make the body. Add **rosemary** leaves for antennae.

23

Delicious drinks

Drinks are **liquids,** which means that they **flow** and **change shape** to fit the glass they are in. Which of these **yummy liquids** is your favorite?

Fizzy float

Add 1 scoop of your favorite **sorbet** (we used raspberry) to a glass of **fizzy lemonade. Watch it fizz!**

Fizzy lemonade is full of carbon dioxide bubbles. The sorbet pushes all the bubbles out of the drink at once.

Monster smoothie

To make a monstrously **green** smoothie, you will need **2 kiwis, 1 apple, half a cucumber**, and **a handful of spinach**. Put all your ingredients into a blender and **blend**!

Blending fruit and veggies cuts them up into tiny pieces. The water inside comes out and the solid ingredients turn into a thick liquid.

Adult ALERT!

Grenadine sinks to the bottom of the glass because it's heavier than orange juice. Scientists call this "density."

Sunset juice

Pour **orange juice** into a glass until it's **nearly full**. **Fill it up** with **grenadine syrup** to make a tropical **sunset**.

Let's get cracking

Eggs come from animals, but most of the eggs that we eat are chicken eggs. There are lots of ways to cook eggs. How do you like yours?

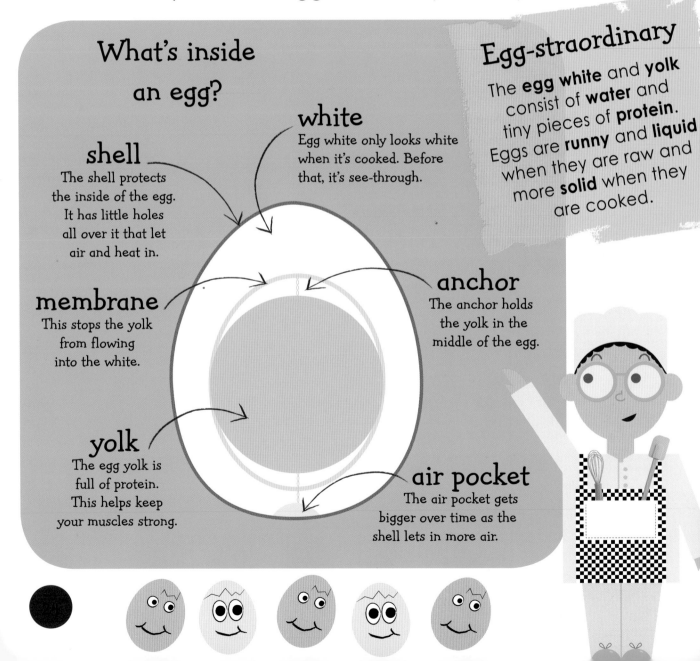

What's inside an egg?

shell
The shell protects the inside of the egg. It has little holes all over it that let air and heat in.

white
Egg white only looks white when it's cooked. Before that, it's see-through.

membrane
This stops the yolk from flowing into the white.

anchor
The anchor holds the yolk in the middle of the egg.

yolk
The egg yolk is full of protein. This helps keep your muscles strong.

air pocket
The air pocket gets bigger over time as the shell lets in more air.

Egg-straordinary

The egg white and yolk consist of water and tiny pieces of protein. Eggs are runny and liquid when they are raw and more solid when they are cooked.

Egg-speriment

As eggs get **older**, the **air pocket** inside gets **bigger**. This makes the egg **float**. **Test** how fresh an egg is by dropping it in water. If it **sinks**, the egg is fresh. If it **floats**, the egg is a little older.

Can you see the tiny holes that let air through the shell?

Only girl chickens lay eggs. Girl chickens are called "hens." Do you know what boy chickens and baby chickens are called?

Animal egg mix-up

It's not just chickens that lay eggs!
Follow the trails to match the egg to the parent.

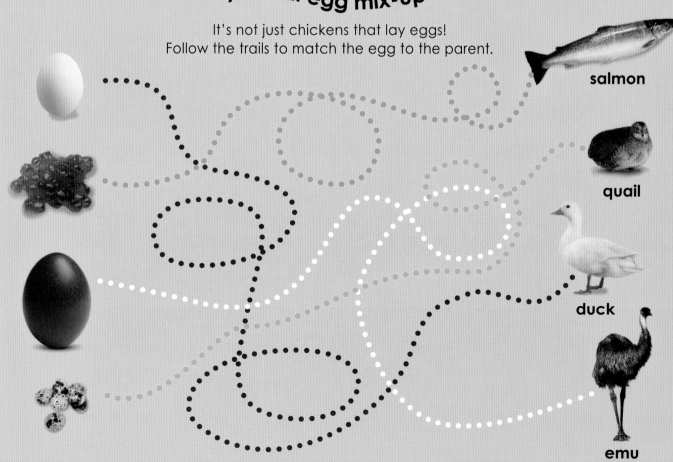

salmon

quail

duck

emu

Happy eggs

Do you like your boiled eggs with a runny yolk or a hard yolk?

Boiled eggs

Gently lower eggs into a pan of **boiling water** using a big spoon. Cook them for **6 minutes** for **soft-boiled eggs**, or **8 minutes** for **hard-boiled eggs**.

A soft-boiled egg will have a runny yolk.

A hard-boiled egg will have a solid yolk.

Adult ALERT!

Chop the top off your eggs with a spoon, and enjoy.

soft-boiled egg

hard-boiled egg

26

Adult ALERT!

Fried egg

Carefully crack an egg into an oiled frying **pan**. Cook it over a **low heat**. Your egg is ready when the white has **completely set** and the yolk is **warm**.

runny egg

Raw egg white is liquid so it spreads to take the shape of the pan. What happens when the white is cooked?

Cooking science

When you **cook** eggs, the pieces of **protein** inside the white and yolk stop floating around. This makes the egg **solidify** (it stops being runny).

Mini meringue mountains

Eggs are great to make desserts **light** and **fluffy** because you can **whip lots of air into them**. These mini meringue mountains are crispy, sweet, and melt in your mouth.

Makes 12 meringues

You will need:

Sugar gives you lots of energy. But too much sugar can be bad for your body, so try not to have too many sweet treats.

2 eggs

½ cup granulated sugar

1

To separate the **egg whites** from the **yolks**, carefully crack the eggs in half. Then tip the yolks **back and forth** between the half shells, letting the whites fall into a **bowl**.

Try not to drop any yolk in the bowl!

crack

egg white

2

Whisk the whites with an electric mixer until they make **stiff peaks**.

sugar

Adult ALERT!

3

Spoon in the sugar, **a little at a time**, and **whisk** until the mixture is completely **smooth**.

Ready!

When the mixture is stiff enough, you'll be able to hold the bowl upside down and nothing will fall out!

Make little meringue mountains.

4 **Spoon** the mixture onto a **baking sheet** to make meringue mountains.

Your meringues should stay as white as possible. If they start to look golden, turn the oven temperature down a little.

5 **Bake** in the oven at 250°F (120°C) for **2 hours**, or until **crispy** all the way through.

Can you see the snowy mountains?

Meringue science

Whisking the egg whites creates foamy **air bubbles** inside. The **sugar** helps to **hold the foam** together, and the **heat** in the oven makes it **dry and crispy**.

SENSE-ible cooking

Can you see the egg whites fluffing up as you whisk?

Can you hear the meringues crunching as you bite them?

Do the raw egg whites and the baked meringue feel very different?

Try your meringue with different fruits and toppings.

Yummy bread

Bread is one of the **most popular foods in the world.** There are lots and lots of **different types** of bread, but this **super-easy recipe** is a delicious one to start with.

You will need:

3¼ cups bread flour

yeast

1 tablespoon fast acting yeast

salt

1 teaspoon salt

Flour is made from a plant called wheat.

oil

2 tablespoons vegetable oil

1¾ cups warm water

Bread is one of the first types of food that humans ever made.

1

In a bowl, **mix** the **flour**, **yeast**, **salt**, **oil**, and **water** until they come together to make a **dough**.

water

yeast

oil

salt

flour

stretch

2

Knead the dough on a floured surface by **stretching**, **folding**, and **squishing** it. Keep kneading for 10 minutes, or until the dough is **springy** but not **sticky**.

Kneading the dough helps make your bread strong.

fold, squish

3

Place the dough on an oiled baking sheet and leave it in a **warm** place for 45 minutes, or until it has **doubled in size**. Preheat the oven to 425°F (220°C).

Watch me get bigger and bigger!

Adult ALERT!

Why does it grow?

Yeast is a very tiny fungus that eats the **sugar** inside the **flour**. When it does, **bubbles** of a gas called carbon dioxide are created and make the bread **rise**.

4

Gently **brush** the dough with warm **water**. This will help make the bread **crusty**.

5 **Bake** in the oven for 30 minutes, or until the bread is cooked **all the way through**. Let it cool down before slicing.

Tap the bottom of your bread. If it's cooked, the air bubbles inside will make it sound hollow.

tap

tap

Adult ALERT!

SENSE-ible cooking

Can you smell your bread baking in the oven?

Can you hear the hollow bubbles inside your bread when you tap it?

Does your bread taste different than the bread you can buy at the store?

Best bruschetta

This tasty **Italian** snack is a great way to enjoy your **delicious bread**. Toast it and top it with **fresh ingredients** that all your **senses** will love.

Makes 4 slices

You will need:

6 tomatoes

Your yummy bread

Tomatoes and garlic are both great at helping your body fight off germs.

4 tablespoons olive oil

1 garlic clove

Season with us!

salt and pepper to season

handful of basil leaves

1

Wash and chop your **tomatoes** and **basil**. Peel your **garlic** clove.

wash

chop

peel

2

Adult ALERT!

Carefully cut **4 slices** from your loaf of **bread**.

Ouch!

lightly toast

3

Lightly **toast** your bread slices in a **pan** or a **toaster**.

Adult ALERT!

4

Rub the **garlic** clove onto your toasted bread to **flavor** it.

Toasting the bread

Heating up the bread creates a **chemical reaction** that changes the **sugar** inside it. This reaction changes the bread's **color**, **texture**, and even **taste**.

38

5

Mmm!

Top your garlic toast with the **chopped tomatoes** and **basil**.

Drizzle
with
olive oil.

SENSE-ible cooking

Can you feel a difference between the bread and the toast?

How does the garlic smell?

Taste your bruschetta before and after seasoning. Which taste do you prefer?

Do you think you could turn toast back into bread?

Season with salt and pepper.

Rainbow ice

When flowy **liquids** get **cold** enough, they **freeze** and turn into stiff **solids**. Try making these frozen **ice pops** to enjoy on a hot sunny day.

I've been frozen upside-down!

Frozen yogurt

Poke a plastic spoon through the lid of a **mini yogurt container**. Leave in the **freezer** overnight. Then pop it out of the container to eat.

fruit juices

yogurt

craft stick

spoon

The warmth from your tongue melts the ice pops.

Layered ice pops

Choose your favorite **fruit juices** and freeze them, **one layer at a time**, in a plastic cup. Once a layer is frozen, **pour** in the next one and **freeze again**. Don't forget the **stick!**

40

See-through pops

Put your favorite **fruit** in an ice pop mold or plastic cup and pour in your **favorite clear drink** (we used lemonade). **Freeze overnight.**

lemonade

fruit

From water to ice

When liquids get cold enough, the tiny pieces inside (molecules) hook onto each other and stop flowing around. The liquid freezes into a solid. Freezing is the opposite of melting.

liquid water

solid ice

Try using a thermometer to check the temperature in your home, outside, in the fridge, and in the freezer.

Temperature

We use "temperature" to **measure** how **hot** or **cold** things are. Water freezes into ice at 32°F (**0°C**), but different liquids freeze and melt at different temperatures.

Chocolate pears

Impress your friends with this **super-scientific**, and super-**tasty, dessert**. It's a great recipe to **experiment** with different **temperatures** and **play** with **flavors**.

Serves 4

You will need:

4 pears (fresh or canned)

5½oz (150g) dark chocolate

4 scoops of vanilla ice cream

¾ cup confectioner's sugar

⅔ cup half and half

1

Carefully **peel** the **pears** and **cut** them in **half**. Remove the **cores** with a spoon.

peeler

scoop scoop

Adult ALERT!

Pears are a great healthy snack because they're full of fiber and vitamins.

2

Break the **chocolate** into **pieces** and place them into a small saucepan.

Snap!

Mmm!

Adult ALERT!

3

Add the **sugar** and **half and half** to the pan and place it over a **very low heat**.

Pour

Dark chocolate has less sugar in it than milk chocolate, so it's a little healthier.

4 Keep **stirring** as the chocolate **melts**, until the sauce is **smooth** and **runny**.

It's getting hot in here.

5 Divide the **pears** between **4 bowls**. Add a scoop of **vanilla ice cream** and top with your **chocolate sauce**.

If the sauce is too chocolatey for you, try stirring in a little more cream.

Adult ALERT!

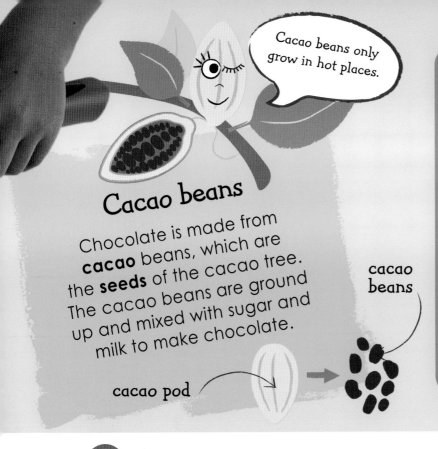

Cacao beans only grow in hot places.

Cacao beans

Chocolate is made from **cacao** beans, which are the **seeds** of the cacao tree. The cacao beans are ground up and mixed with sugar and milk to make chocolate.

cacao pod

cacao beans

SENSE-ible cooking

What happens when the hot chocolate sauce touches the cold ice cream?

Does the sauce smell very chocolatey?

Taste some ice cream with and without the chocolate sauce. How is it different?

A melty experiment

When chocolate gets hot enough, it turns from a hard solid into a flowy liquid. You can experiment to find out how hot chocolate needs to be to melt. What happens when you put a piece of chocolate...

Dark chocolate, milk chocolate, and white chocolate are made differently. They melt at different temperatures.

...in the fridge.

...in your hand.

...on your tongue.

...outside in the sun.

...outside in the shade.

Look, you're a cook!

Chefs rely on their senses and skills to follow a set of **steps** when they cook. Think about your own cooking. Can you follow **the chef's steps?**

Use your senses

All of your **senses** work as a **team** to help you enjoy your food. Think about your **favorite** recipes. What **smells, textures, colors,** and **sounds** made them so **special?**

Make it yummy

Try to **taste** your ingredients **as you cook. Play** and **experiment** with recipes to make them your own. How can you make your food taste **even better?**

Stay safe

Chefs have to be **careful** in the kitchen. Always ask an **adult** to cook with you, and make sure to **wash your hands** with **soap** before you begin.

What's your favorite food? Why?

Be creative

Chefs love to **make up** new recipes. Start with your **favorite ingredients** and **create** your very own dish. What will you **name** it?

46

Good job!

....
(Write your name here.)

 is a cook!

Index